Wombats

Wombats

Mary Berendes

THE CHILD'S WORLD, INC.

Library of Congress Cataloging-in-Publication Data
Berendes, Mary.
    Wombats / by Mary Berendes
        p.   cm.
    Includes index.
    Summary: Describes the physical characteristics, behavior,
habitat, and life cycle of common and hairy-nosed wombats.
    ISBN 1-56766-482-2 (lib. bdg. : alk. paper)
    1. Wombats—Juvenile literature.   [1. Wombats.]   I. Title.
        QL737.M39B47   1998
        599.2'4—dc21   97-33249
                                CIP
                                AC

Photo Credits

ANIMALS ANIMALS © Adrienne T. Gibson: 15
ANIMALS ANIMALS © Fritz Prenzel: 23
ANIMALS ANIMALS © Kathy Atkinson: 26
ANIMALS ANIMALS © Mickey Gibson: 10
ANIMALS ANIMALS © Steven David Miller: 24
© Art Wolfe/Tony Stone Images: 29
© Chad Ehlers/Tony Stone Images: 9
© Dean Lee/The Wildlife Collection: 2, 16, 20
© Franklin J. Viola/Comstock, Inc.: 19
© Martin Harvey/The Wildlife Collection: cover, 6, 13, 30

On the cover...

Front cover: This *southern hairy-nosed wombat* is looking for food.
Page 2: This young *common wombat* is playing in the grass.

Table of Contents

As the sun sets over the Australian forest, many creatures come out to eat and play. Bats swoop from caves and frogs croak happily. Soon an animal can be heard crashing through the bushes. Sticks break and leaves rustle. Suddenly a small, round creature appears. What could it be? It's a wombat!

What Are Wombats?

Wombats belong to a group of animals called **marsupials**. Marsupials are animals that have a pocket of skin for carrying their babies. This pocket is called a **pouch**. Only female marsupials have pouches. A female wombat's pouch is underneath her body. Kangaroos and koalas are marsupials, too.

Common wombats like this one have short fur. ⇒

What Do Wombats Look Like?

Many people think of wombats as cute and cuddly. But they are really very strong. Their bodies are almost all muscle! Wombats are diggers. They use their strong bodies to scoop and kick dirt until they are far underground. They have short, powerful legs to dig into the hard dirt. Their strong, flat claws loosen the dirt to make digging easier.

Wombats grow to be about three feet long. Many wombats weigh about 40 pounds, but some weigh over 75 pounds. About one million years ago, there was a giant wombat that was as big as a hippo!

⇐ Wombats like this one have strong legs for digging.

Are Wombats Smart?

Many people think wombats are clumsy and slow, but that is not true. Wombats are very smart. They like to play and run. They are also very careful and alert. Wombats pay attention to everything they smell or see. They listen carefully to make sure an area is safe before they enter it. If they get scared or angry, wombats can run as fast as 25 miles an hour.

This hairy-nosed wombat is looking for things to eat. ⇒

Where Do Wombats Live?

Wombats live only in Australia and Tasmania. They live in **burrows**, or tunnels, that they dig in the sides of hills. The end of a wombat's burrow usually has a **den**, or resting place. The den is lined with dry grass and leaves. That is where the wombat sleeps and raises its babies.

Wombats live only in areas that have very hot summers and lots of dry weather. Nighttime is more comfortable in these hot areas, so wombats are **nocturnal**. That means they go out mostly at night. At night, the wombats can play and eat without getting hot or tired. They also do not have to worry about many enemies. That is because most of their enemies are sound asleep!

This wombat is coming out of its den as the sun goes down. ⇒

Are There Different Kinds of Wombats?

There are two kinds of wombats. The *common wombat* lives in forests. Its burrows are in hillsides, near creeks and ditches. Common wombats have thick, coarse fur that is brown or gray. They also have short, rounded ears. Common wombats are calm when they are young, but they can be dangerous when they grow up.

⇐ This young common wombat is sniffing the air.

The *hairy-nosed wombat* lives on the flat grasslands. It gets its name from the short hairs on its nose. It has a large, square face and long, pointed ears. Its gray fur is very soft and silky. Hairy-nosed wombats are very rare. Many of them now live in a protected park. There they are safe and have plenty of food.

This hairy-nosed wombat lives in a zoo where it is safe. ⇒

Wombats eat grasses, roots, and the bark of trees and bushes. They have four front teeth that they use for cutting and biting. These teeth are a lot like a beaver's teeth. But wombats do not use their teeth to cut down trees. Instead, they use them to gently nibble and bite their food.

⇐ This common wombat is searching in the grass for food.   21

A wombat's front teeth never stop growing. Every time the wombat bites something, it wears down the teeth. If the wombat could not find things to chew on, its teeth would become too long. Then it might have trouble eating the foods it needs to stay healthy. For wombats, chewing and nibbling are very important.

This hungry wombat has found some leaves to eat. ⇒

How Are Baby Wombats Born?

Most of the time, wombats like to live alone. But when it is time to mate, wombats leave their burrows and search for other wombats. When a wombat is looking for a mate, it makes a low, growling sound. To people, a wombat's call sounds like an animal coughing. But to another wombat, this sound means "Here I am!"

⇐ This wombat has come out of its den to look for a mate.

Baby wombats are very different from other animal babies. When a newborn wombat comes out of its mother, it is very tiny—about as big as a jellybean! The newborn has no fur on its body. It cannot even see or hear. But it does have strong legs for crawling. Right after it is born, the baby crawls into its mother's pouch. There it is safe and warm.

Once the baby is inside the pouch, it hangs onto something that looks like a little finger. This is called a **teat**. Milk from the mother's body comes out of the teat. That is what the baby drinks while it is inside the pouch. Slowly, the baby wombat grows bigger and stronger. After about six months, it is ready to leave the pouch.

⇐ This little wombat is already seven months old.

Do Wombats Have Any Enemies?

Since wombats are nocturnal, they do not have many enemies. Wild dogs called *dingoes* sometimes eat them, but most of the time, wombats are left alone. When a dingo attacks a strong, angry wombat, it is in for a long fight.

The biggest danger to wombats is people. People are destroying the areas where wombats live. Cows and sheep that people raise are eating the grasses wombats need. Some farmers even trap and kill wombats that chew through their fences and eat their crops.

Dingoes like this one sometimes like to eat wombats. ⇒

Some wombats may be pests, but most stay far away from people. They are happiest when they are alone in their burrows or munching green grass. Maybe one day you will travel to Australia. If you do, listen for a noisy creature in the bushes. Perhaps you will see a furry wombat taking its nighttime walk!

Glossary

burrows (BUR–rowz)
Burrows are tunnels that wombats make underground. Some burrows are very long.

den (DEN)
A den is a space where an animal rests and raises its babies. A wombat's den is usually at the end of its burrow.

marsupial (mar-SOO-pee-ull)
A marsupial is an animal that carries its young in a pouch. Wombats, kangaroos, and koalas are all marsupials.

nocturnal (nok–TUR–null)
Nocturnal animals come out mostly at night. Wombats, owls, and bats are all nocturnal.

pouch (POWCH)
A pouch is a pocket of skin where marsupial babies live. It is on the mother's stomach.

teat (TEET)
A wombat mother produces milk from a teat. It is like a baby bottle inside her pouch.

Index